Young
Mark Twain

Young Mark Twain

by Louis Sabin
illustrated by Ray Burns

Troll Associates

Library of Congress Cataloging-in-Publication Data

Sabin, Louis.
   Young Mark Twain / by Louis Sabin; illustrated by Ray Burns.
     p.   cm.
   Summary: A brief biography with emphasis on the early years of the
noted author and humorist.
    ISBN 0-8167-1783-4 (lib. bdg.)   ISBN 0-8167-1784-2 (pbk.)
    1. Twain, Mark, 1835-1910—Biography—Youth—Juvenile literature.
2. Authors, American—19th century—Biography—Juvenile literature.
3. Humorists, American—19th century—Biography—Juvenile
literature. [1. Twain, Mark, 1835-1910—Childhood and youth.
2. Authors, American.] I. Burns, Raymond, 1924-   , ill. II. Title.
PS1332.S26 1990
818'.409—dc20
[B]
[92]   89-33982

Young
Mark Twain

Across America, thousands of heads tilted upward toward the sky. Something rare and marvelous was coming that day in November 1835—Halley's comet. Everyone had heard about it. The last time its fiery tail had been seen blazing across the sky was in 1758. Halley's comet traveled around the sun about every seventy-seven years. Only when the comet neared the sun could it be seen from earth.

Among the excited sky watchers in the village of Florida, Missouri, were Jane and John Clemens. They stood with their children in the cold November night. This was a moment none of them wanted to miss.

"Papa," said ten-year-old Orion, "when the new baby comes, we can call it Halley. That's a good name for a girl or boy."

"No, son," Mr. Clemens said. "That's a fine name, but your mother and I have the names already picked out."

"And fine names they are," Mrs. Clemens said. "If it's a girl, she'll be called Sarah. If it's a boy, he'll be called Samuel."

Halley's comet was still thrilling America when Samuel Langhorne Clemens was born on November 30, 1835. He was a weak baby and very small. The family did not expect him to live through the winter. Back then, many babies died before their first birthday. With no hospitals, no modern lifesaving medicines, and no nurseries with special equipment, the threat of death hung over every newborn child.

But Little Sam, as the family called the tiny red-haired baby, was a survivor. To the surprise of everyone, he got through that first difficult year. And he went on surprising people all his life. For Samuel Clemens—or Mark Twain, as the world would one day know him—had the kind of brilliance that outshone any comet.

Little Sam was born in a small frame house. It had just two rooms, and a kitchen in an attached shed. Even though the Clemens's house was small and crowded, it was one of the best in the village. Most of the other houses were simple log cabins. Even the village church was a log cabin.

Mark Twain remembered this church well. The cracks between its logs were wide enough for winter winds to whistle through. The church floor was made of puncheons. (A puncheon is half a split log.) These split logs were arranged flat side up.

"The cracks between the logs were not filled," Twain later wrote. "If you dropped anything smaller than a peach, it was likely to go through."

The church floor was raised off the ground, leaving two or three feet of open space underneath. This open space made a pleasant shelter for pigs from a nearby farm. They lay under the church, snuffling and grunting in their sleep. Nobody minded that. But wandering dogs sometimes pestered the pigs. That made an awful racket.

When it happened during Sunday services, the preacher's voice got louder and louder. But he was fighting a losing battle. He had to wait until someone chased the dogs and the pigs away from the church. Mark Twain never forgot this. It was a lot more fun than icy winds coming up through the floor in winter and fleas coming up through the floor in summer.

Adults, however, suffered these discomforts only once a week. The children suffered them every weekday, because the church was also the schoolhouse. The slab benches, made of cut logs, were pews on Sunday and classroom seats the rest of the time. There were no desks or any other kinds of school equipment. Each pupil brought a slate and learned to write on that.

Florida, Missouri, had just two streets. Each one stretched about the length of two football fields. There were also a few lanes. These were rough paths winding through the cornfields. Neither the two streets nor the lanes were paved. They were dirt roads and not bad in good weather. But any rain turned them into ankle-deep mud. And a few dry days made them thick with dust.

When Mark Twain was an adult, he was famous for wearing all-white suits and shoes. He took great pride in looking spotlessly clean—something that would have been impossible back home.

John Clemens, Sam's father, was a lawyer and shopkeeper. But he wasn't very successful at either line of work. Before the family had moved to Florida, Missouri, Mr. Clemens had tried to make a living in several Tennessee and Kentucky towns. But he failed in all of them. So when John Quarles, his brother-in-law, invited him to become a business partner in Florida, Missouri, John Clemens gladly accepted.

Mr. Quarles owned the village general store. It sold cotton cloth, salt mackerel, groceries, vegetables, coffee, sugar, brooms, farm tools, men's hats, ladies' bonnets, and candleholders and other cheap tin products. The store also stocked buckshot, gunpowder, nails, molasses, cheese, and corn whiskey.

Prices at the general store were low. For ten cents, a customer could buy a bushel of apples, peaches, potatoes, or corn. Butter was six cents a pound; sugar and coffee cost five cents a pound each. A plump chicken for roasting sold for a dime, while eggs went for three cents a dozen.

Even though the prices were low, many customers could not afford to pay for what they needed. They rarely had any money. Instead, they traded with the shopkeeper. A farmer might trade a couple of sides of bacon for a needed tool or exchange a bushel of corn for some coffee. The store did more business trading with customers than in actual cash sales.

Customers who paid cash got a bonus. As Mark Twain later wrote, "If a boy bought five or ten cents' worth of anything, he was entitled to half a handful of sugar from the barrel. If a woman bought a few yards of calico, she was entitled to a spool of thread . . . ."

After a while, John Clemens lost interest in shopkeeping and went back to practicing law. He was well liked by his neighbors, and they elected him justice of the peace. A justice of the peace acts as a judge in small cases.

As justice of the peace for Florida, Missouri, Mr. Clemens settled disputes between neighbors, decided cases involving petty theft or disturbance of the peace, and saw that village laws were obeyed. The villagers soon started calling him "Judge," a title he kept all his life. John Clemens was the real-life model on which Mark Twain based the character of Judge Thatcher in *The Adventures of Tom Sawyer.*

Still, there was not very much work for a lawyer in the tiny village. So in 1839, the Clemens family moved to Hannibal, Missouri. Hannibal was a small town on the west bank of the Mississippi River. It was a stopping place for steamboats carrying goods up and down the river. Local farmers brought their harvests to Hannibal. From there, the goods could be sent downstream to St. Louis, Memphis, and New Orleans, or upstream to Dubuque, Minneapolis, and St. Paul.

The steamboats carried passengers as well as merchandise. There were business people, river-boat gamblers, traveling entertainers, settlers moving west, and visitors from foreign lands. There were good people and bad people, rich and poor, educated and uneducated, rough and gentle.

Every steamboat stop along the river was
enriched by a colorful variety of people. The
steamboats meant romance, adventure, and
escape. Every youngster who lived along the river
dreamed of working on board one of those grand
vessels.

Sam Clemens was four years old when the family settled in Hannibal. It didn't take him long to fall in love with the Mississippi and with the steamboats traveling its waters. The arrival of a steamboat was a thrilling moment. From the distance came the loud whistle. Then shouts echoed throughout the town: "Steamboat's a-comin'!" It was a signal for the children of Hannibal to race down the hilly streets to the pier. Their excitement was picked up by all the dogs in town, who barked wildly as they ran alongside the children.

The adults, who wanted to seem dignified, walked slowly down to the river. But they were excited too. And when the boat rounded the bend in the river, its passengers were treated to a hearty welcome from almost the entire population of Hannibal. Nothing in the life of Hannibal or young Sam Clemens matched the joy felt when a riverboat steamed in.

As Mark Twain, Sam Clemens recorded his life in Hannibal and his love of the river in book after book. We read about Tom Sawyer and his friend Huckleberry Finn riding their raft down the mighty Mississippi. The character of Tom Sawyer was based on Sam himself. And Tom Blankenship, a close boyhood friend of Sam Clemens, was the real-life model for the character of Huck Finn.

Tom Blankenship usually had to fend for himself. The boy wandered around town and often got into one scrape after another. He slept in a barrel in his ramshackle home. While Mrs. Clemens sent Sam off to school, Tom Blankenship went fishing, hunted turtle eggs, and wandered through the surrounding woods. Like Huck Finn, Tom was pitied by grown-ups and envied by the children.

Readers of *The Adventures of Tom Sawyer* also know that Becky Thatcher is Tom Sawyer's girlfriend. She is sweet and kind, admires Tom's daring, and laughs at his jokes. Becky Thatcher was likewise based on a real-life model. She was Laura Hawkins, who lived right across from Sam's house on Hill Street. Laura, who was two years older than Sam, always remembered the slow, funny way he talked. She also remembered that Sam was a real trial to his mother because he often played hooky from school.

Sam Clemens's problems in school began early on. He was enrolled in a small log-cabin schoolhouse. In those days, there were no public schools in Missouri. But there were two private schools in Hannibal. Both charged twenty-five cents a week for each student.

As Mark Twain wrote, "I remember an episode on that first day. I broke one of the rules and was warned not to do it again. I was told that the penalty for a second breach was a whipping. I presently broke the rule again, and my teacher told me to go out and find a switch and fetch it."

Sam was pleased that his teacher sent him and no other to get the switch. Because after a few minutes outside, he found the perfect "whip"—a flimsy wood shaving found near the barrel maker's shop. "I carried it to my teacher," Twain wrote, "presented it, and stood before her in an attitude of meekness and resignation, which seemed to me calculated to win favor and sympathy. But it did not happen."

Sam's teacher looked at the thin, soft wood shaving and said she would choose someone with better judgment. "It saddens me yet to remember," Twain wrote, "how many faces lighted up with the hope of getting that appointment. Jim Dunlap got it. And when he returned with the switch of his choice, I recognized that he was an expert."

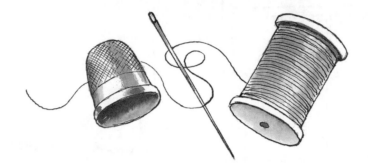

The whipping Sam received was painful, but he remained as mischievous as ever. He was always getting into trouble. When a snake or some large bugs turned up in another student's desk, it was sure to be Sam Clemens who put them there. He cracked jokes, made faces, squirmed, and daydreamed.

After two years in the log-cabin school, Sam went to Mr. Cross's school. Sam's behavior was no better there. If anything, he was more trouble than before. When the weather was warm enough, Sam headed for the swimming hole instead of the schoolhouse.

In an attempt to stop him, Mrs. Clemens sewed Sam's shirt closed at the collar every morning. That way, she would know if he took off his shirt during the day. If the thread was broken, it meant Sam had taken a dip in the swimming hole. But if the collar was still sewn closed by evening, Mrs. Clemens felt sure that Sam had gone to school.

One night, Mrs. Clemens checked the sewing and was satisfied. But Sam's younger brother Henry said, "Ma, look at the sewing again. Didn't you use white thread this morning? And isn't that black thread where the white thread was?"

Mrs. Clemens was furious with Sam, and Sam was furious with Henry. Sam was so angry that he threw mud at his younger brother. But that only made matters worse. Now Sam's mother had two reasons to punish him.

Like Aunt Polly in *The Adventures of Tom Sawyer,* Mrs. Clemens used extra chores as punishment. One of these chores was for Sam to whitewash the picket fence around the house. One time, it happened on a really beautiful Saturday. Sam's friends passed by with their fishing poles and cans of worms, heading for a great day at the river.

More than anything, Sam wanted to go with his
friends. As they stood laughing at him, he had a
great idea. Sam pretended that going fishing was
nothing much, but that whitewashing a fence was
the greatest fun in the world. He acted sorry for
the boys, because they didn't have the special
treat that he was having. Sam's acting was so
good that the boys begged to be allowed to work
on the fence.

At first, Sam said no. Then, as if he were doing
them a favor, he agreed to let each one have a

turn—for a price. The boys had to trade their
treasures—fishing worms, doorknobs, live frogs,
and other special things they were carrying—to
get their turns. With all the boys working, the
whitewashing was done quickly. Then the boys
went off, with Sam merrily leading the way, for
a day of fishing. Mrs. Clemens could only marvel
at how swiftly young Sam had whitewashed the
fence. And readers could only laugh when they
read the whitewashing episode in *The Adventures
of Tom Sawyer*.

Mrs. Clemens, however, wasn't often fooled by Sam. She knew he was a cutup, but she also knew that he wasn't a mean or bad boy. To her, Sam's lengthy reasons for missing school, tearing his clothing, being late for supper, and getting into other kinds of mischief were just plain funny. One day, a neighbor asked Mrs. Clemens if she could ever believe anything Sam told her.

"He is the wellspring of truth," Mrs. Clemens answered, "but you can't bring up the whole well with one bucket. I know his average. Therefore, he never deceives me. I discount ninety percent of what he says for embroidery. What is left is perfect and priceless truth, without a flaw in it anywhere."

From the age of seven through thirteen, Sam Clemens spent his summers at his uncle John Quarles's farm. As far as Sam was concerned, the farm was heaven. All his life he remembered the beauty of the woods there, the sounds of the birds and other animals, the colors of nature, and the taste of wild grapes, blackberries, hazelnuts, and persimmons.

There were so many rules for Sam to obey back home in Hannibal, but there was complete freedom for the children at the farm. No need for shoes or collars, no jackets to keep clean, and no special time to get up or go to bed.

For Sam, farm life was different from town life in another way. Nobody put on airs at the farm. Nobody showed off wealth or property or family background. At the farm, a person was judged by what was done, not by what was owned or inherited. This love of simplicity and honesty stayed with Sam Clemens the rest of his life.

Even though Sam avoided school a lot, he was a fast learner and a good reader. He also took pride in a medal he won for being the best speller in Mr. Cross's school. When he was much older and very famous for his writing, Mark Twain was asked how he had learned to write so well if he went to school so little. With a twinkle in his eye, Twain said that was the way he remembered it. But he added that when he was younger, he could remember anything—whether it happened or not.

So maybe young Sam Clemens wasn't absent from school quite as much as he liked people to think. In any case, what was absolutely true about Mark Twain—boy and man—was that he could tell a mighty good story!

In 1847, when Sam Clemens was eleven, his father died. Now it was up to the children to look after their mother. Sam left school and became an apprentice to Joseph Ament, publisher of the Hannibal *Courier*. As an apprentice, Sam had to light the stove that heated the office, bring in water from the outside pump, and sweep the floor. Then he had to sort and set type, wet down the paper stock, keep all equipment clean, wrap 350 newspapers to be mailed, and hand-deliver another 100 copies.

For all this, Sam received his meals, a bed in the shop, and two suits a year. He did not receive any pay, and he didn't even get new suits. Mr. Ament just passed on some of his old clothing to Sam. It was worn out and far too big for the boy. As Twain later reported, "His shirts gave me the uncomfortable sense of living in a circus tent, and I had to turn up his pants to my ears to make them short enough."

Sam left the *Courier* in 1850 and went to work for his older brother Orion. An experienced printer, Orion had been working in St. Louis. He came back to Hannibal, bought a weekly newspaper called the Hannibal *Journal,* and hired Sam for $3.50 a week, plus room and board.

At that time, $3.50 was good pay. But Sam didn't see a penny of it. The newspaper never made a profit, and Orion never had the money to pay Sam. After struggling for a few years, the *Journal* stopped publication.

Even so, the time spent working for Orion wasn't a total loss for Sam. It was his debut as a writer. He wrote news stories—whether the events in them happened or not. He made fun of the town's other newspaper in humorous stories. Now and then, he even threw in a poem. And Sam made up his own letters to the editor, then answered them.

Once, when Orion was out of town, Sam filled the newspaper with so many attention-getting items that the number of subscriptions zoomed. But it also brought threats of lawsuits and worse. Sam was told to stick to printing from then on.

In 1853, when the *Journal* folded, Sam Clemens set out on his own. Now eighteen years old, he was a competent printer, and he knew he could get work anywhere. So off he went, first to St. Louis, then to New York, Philadelphia, Washington, D.C., Cincinnati, and anywhere else the mood carried him. Wherever he went, Sam found work as a printer. He also continued writing, selling his articles for two or three dollars to newspapers and magazines.

After four years of moving from city to city, Sam Clemens decided to go to South America to seek his fortune. So he boarded the riverboat *Paul Jones* and headed down the Mississippi for New Orleans. There, he would get on another ship for South America. But as he was traveling down the Mississippi, Sam changed his mind. He asked Horace Bixby, the pilot of the riverboat, to teach him to pilot.

Bixby liked Sam and agreed to take him on as an apprentice pilot. Sam, in turn, agreed to pay Bixby five hundred dollars for this instruction. But all Sam had with him was one hundred dollars, enough to cover the passage to South America. The other four hundred dollars would have to come out of Sam's future earnings on the river.

Sam soon learned to navigate the tricky waters of the Mississippi. He memorized every turn and bend of the river. He also listened with fascination to hundreds of stories about river people. These included adventures, crimes, heroic deeds, and virtually everything that happened along the route of the *Paul Jones*. As Mark Twain, Sam Clemens told all about his experiences on the river in *Life on the Mississippi*, one of his finest books.

Sam Clemens first took the pen name of Mark Twain in 1863. At that time, an old river pilot named Isaiah Sellers was writing a column for the New Orleans *Picayune*. He told about the Mississippi and the river's steamboats. The column, however, was overloaded with facts and boringly written. Sam couldn't resist poking fun at it. So he wrote an article that humorously imitated Sellers's column, and he sent it to the New Orleans *Daily Crescent*.

Sam's article was printed under the by-line of "Mark Twain," a name he took from the river-boat cry "mark twain!" It means that the water is two fathoms, or twelve feet, deep. In river talk, that tells pilots it is safe for their boats to move forward without touching bottom.

From then on, he was less and less Sam Clemens and more and more Mark Twain. The name became famous as he continued to write humorous articles and stories. Many of them were about the places Twain visited both in the United States and abroad. He even made it finally to South America.

Twain's success and popularity reached the point where he was a celebrity to the entire English-reading world. Even England's renowned Oxford University gave him an honorary degree. True to character, though, Mark Twain thought the degree was a big joke. He knew his school record was far from the best.

On April 20, 1910, Halley's comet reappeared
in the sky. It hadn't been seen with the naked eye
since November 1835. One day later, April 21,
1910, Mark Twain died. He was seventy-four
years old. His life practically began and ended
with an appearance by Halley's comet. The year
before his death, Twain spoke about this. His wit
was as sharp as ever. "The Almighty has no doubt
said, 'Now here go those two frauds. They came
in together, and they must go out together.' Oh,
I'm looking forward to that." Mark Twain's last
story was told.